lown
Tales
ERNEST ARI

This edition published in 1989 by
Tiger Books International PLC, London

ISBN 1-870461-79-7

Printed and bound in Hungary

THE BRAMBLEDOWN TALES

HENRY HEDGEHOG'S HAT

TIGER BOOKS INTERNATIONAL
LONDON

One or two strange discoveries

Chapter One

A HAPPY END

Somewhere between here and there stands the village of Brambledown. Do you know it? On a spring morning, when the sun smiles between the hills, you can hear the sounds of Brambledown waking up – alarm clocks ringing, people yawning, curtains swished, windows opening. In the woods and fields, the animals wake up too. The birds sing, the cats stretch, the cows want to be milked.

Between the roots of a tree, snug under a quilt of leaves, Henry Hedgehog woke up one spring morning, with a snuffle and a scratch. He was not just waking up after one night's sleep: he had been asleep all winter. So he was *very* hungry indeed. Henry set off to look for breakfast. And on the way he made one or two strange discoveries.

He found that the kittens had grown into cats. He found that the cygnets had grown up into swans. He found that the calves had grown into cows and the foals into horses. "What a lot I've missed while I was asleep," he thought.

"When I dozed off last autumn, the trees were bare and the river was hard with ice. Now there are so many leaves on the trees that I can't see the sky, and the river is all bubbly. What a lot I've missed while I was asleep," he thought.

"When I nodded off last autumn, the animals were all wearing their heavy winter coats. Now they are wearing their spring clothes. What a lot I've missed while I was asleep . . ." he thought, "and *why don't I have any new spring clothes*!"

Then an awful idea came to Henry. "Maybe I overslept! Maybe the animals who don't go to sleep all winter like I do have eaten everything eatable in the whole world!"

"Oh dear! Oh dear! Oh dear! It's not fair! Oh dear! Poor me! No spring clothes and no breakfast!"

"Good morning, you lazy lie-abed!" called a cheery voice. It was Barney Brown the rabbit. "I was wondering when you would stir yourself and wake up, Henry."

"What news? What news? What have I missed?" asked Henry eagerly. "What's been happening in Brambledown?"

"Oh this and that. Something and nothing," said Barney. "There is one piece of news . . . but I expect you've heard it already."

"No! What is it? What is it?"

"It's just that Sabrina and Sam Squirrel are getting married. And *everybody* in Brambledown is invited to the wedding. Will you be going?"

"Good morning!" called Barney

Barney said, "You don't look very pleased to hear the news."

"Herrumph," said Henry. "How can I go to a wedding without any new spring clothes? Now please excuse me. I haven't eaten a bite all winter."

Henry found some breakfast after all. It was spring and there was plenty to go round, even for people who overslept. Henry found something else, too.

Sitting under the bramble hedge was the strangest little stranger he had ever seen in Brambledown. It was something like a person, but very small, with a tangle of hair and big round eyes.

"Morning," said Henry, as friendly as can be. But shall I tell you what he was thinking? "*If I had a top hat like that, I wouldn't let it lie in the wet grass.*"

The stranger said nothing. "Perhaps he's deaf," thought Henry and went closer.

"I said, *GOOD MORNING*!"

Still the stranger said nothing. Can you guess why? It was a child's rag doll left behind after a picnic.

"How rude!" thought Henry. "He's not asleep, because his eyes are open." And he gave the little stranger a push which sent him sprawling. "Ah! Ha ha! Silly me! It's not a person at all! It's a baby scarecrow . . . And here, if I'm not mistaken, is my new spring outfit!" He coughed politely. "Excuse me, sir, but I see a rather fine top hat in the grass beside you. Is it yours?" The doll, of course, said nothing.

The strangest little stranger

"Or are you using it?"

Nothing.

"Could I try it for size?"

Nothing.

So Henry picked up the hat and put it on. It was just the right size.

Henry . . . feeling rather proud of himself

Chapter Two

HENRY'S PRIDE AND JOY

"You mean I can have it for my very own?" Henry asked the little doll who was sitting under the hedge.

The doll, of course, said nothing. So Henry thanked him very much and marched away wearing the hat.

"How very smart I must look!" thought Henry. "It's just the right size for me, and so very elegant! I don't suppose there is a single hedgehog in Brambledown who has such a fine hat. In fact, I don't suppose there is a single animal in Brambledown who has such a fine hat. In fact, I don't suppose there is a single animal in the whole wide world who has such a fine hat!"

As you can see. Henry was feeling rather proud of himself.

Ronnie Rook
called out

From high up in the trees, Ronnie Rook saw Henry swaggering along the forest path in his high hat. He gave a loud whistle and called out, in his creaking voice,

"*How* d'you do, Henry!
How do you do, Henry!"

But all Henry said in reply was "Herrumph!" And he went on his way with his pink, pointed nose in the air.

"*How* d'you do, Henry! *How* d'you do!"

"Herrumph!"

"Aw dear! Aw dear!" cawed Ronnie. "I think somebody is feeling rather too grand this morning. *Just* because he's found himself a hat."

There is something very funny about a haughty hedgehog in a high hat, so Ronnie flew off to ell all the other birds in the wood what he had seen.

Henry went back the way he had come. He passed by Barney Brown's burrow again. The rabbit had to look once and look twice before he recognized his old friend. Then he stared and stared. After all, a haughty hedgehog in a high hat is a very unusual sight.

"Hi, Henry!
Where did you get that
Where did you get that
Where did you get that hat!"

But all that Henry said in reply was, "Herrumph!" and went on his way with his pink, pointed nose in the air.

"So-ho! Is that the way of it!" thought Barney Brown. "I see somebody is feeling very grand this morning because of his new hat." And he called out for his wife to come and see the new Henry Hedgehog. "Come up and look at this, my dear Mrs Brown!"

Barney Brown stared

Mrs Brown stared too

Mrs Brown bustled out of her burrow and stared after Henry Hedgehog.

"How smart you look, Henry! Did you buy the hat specially for the wedding?" she called after him.

But all Henry said in reply was, "Herrumph!" and went on his way with his pink, pointed nose held high in the air.

"Do you see what I see, Mrs Brown?" said Barney.

"I do see what you see, Mr Brown," said his wife. "I see a hedgehog who has grand ideas *in* his head just because he has a grand hat *on* his head. And I call it a sorry shame, because Henry was such a very *agreeable* hedgehog when he had no high hat and no high-and-mighty ideas."

It was the same wherever Henry went in Brambledown.

The longer he wore his hat, the grander he felt. And every time one of his friends called out to him, "Hi, Henry! That's a fine hat you have on!" he only said,

"Herrumph!"

and pushed his pink, pointed nose even higher into the air.

In fact, by the time he reached the wheat field and passed by the house of the Field-Mouse Family, his nose was so high in the air that his hat fell off and rolled down his back and bowled along the ground. He had to run after it to get it back. And *that* was not a very grand thing to do.

As he brushed off the dust and put back on his hat, he heard a giggling and a tittering in among the tall stalks of wheat. It was the little children of Mr and Mrs Field-Mouse who were watching him chase his fancy hat.

His hat rolled down his back

Field-Mouse found it funny

They were laughing at Henry and his high-and-mighty hat. "You ought to tie it on with a piece of string under your chin!" squeaked Fenella Field-Mouse.

"Or with ribbons!" shrieked Fergus Field-Mouse. "Nice pink ribbons!"

Of course Henry did not laugh. He was much too grand to laugh at himself. He pretended not to hear the mice giggling, and went on his way with his pink, pointed nose so high in the air that he could not see where he was going at all. He stumbled over stones. He fell over fir-cones. He tripped over tree roots. And the owls hooted and the rooks rocked with laughter and the frogs croaked and the horses hinnied. But still Henry refused to even smile. He was much too high and mighty.

Even the littlest mouse

Ronnie Rook told Barney Brown all about it, and together they laughed and laughed.

"Oh dear! Oh dear! Is there anything in the world so funny as a haughty hedgehog in a high hat? Ha ha ha!"

They laughed and laughed

But in their heart of hearts, the animals of Brambledown were a little bit *jealous* of Henry Hedgehog's hat. They wished they had hats to wear to the wedding of Sam and Sabrina Squirrel. They wished they had something to make them feel so grand that they walked with their noses in the air, as proud as proud can be.

Even so, they were very sorry to hear their friend Henry say, "Herrumph!" and go on his way.

"Where can we go to get hats?"

Chapter Three

HOW TO GET HATS

"Why should Henry be the only one with a hat?" they began to say. "Why can't we all have hats? Where can we go to get hats?"

They asked Mr Wise-Owl, but he only said, "Who knows? Who knows?"

"That's what we asked *you*," complained the animals.

"I know what," said Maurice Mole. "Let's ask Hoppity Hare. He's quite mad, but full of good ideas." So they struggled up to the top of High Hill and found Hoppity Hare practising his long-jump. He landed with a thumpety-thump and looked up in surprise.

"Hoppity-woppity! What a lot of visitors! Did I invite you to tea? Is there a party? Is it my birthday?"

"Please, Hoppity. How can we get hats?"

"Hoppity-woppity! Hats? Why? Is it raining? Is it hailing on your heads?"

So they explained about Henry Hedgehog's hat and how they all wanted to look grand for the Squirrel wedding. Hoppity sat very still for a long time. In fact he sat so still for so long that everybody thought he had gone to sleep. But just as they began to creep away, he opened his eyes and leapt up: "I've thought about it! There are three ways to get hats. First you can make them – out of saucepans and bottles and such."

"Don't have any saucepans!"

"But we don't have any saucepans or bottles."

"Well then, you can go down into Brambledown Village and steal hats off hat racks. You could climb up water pipes and take them down from wardrobes and out from under beds."

The animals turned very pale indeed.

"I don't *climb*," said Maurice Mole, "I burrow. And I think it would be very wicked to steal a hat, anyway."

"I don't *climb*," said Maurice

"And *very* dangerous," said Susie Squirrel.

"*Very*, *very* dangerous!" said Fergus Field-Mouse.

"Well then," said Hoppity Hare, "You can simply wait for the wind to blow."

If you wonder how Hoppity came to know so much about hats, remember! He lives at the top of a hill. From there, he can look down into the village and the fields and along the road. And he has seen with his sharp brown eyes what happens to hats when a gale begins to blow.

"Thank you Hoppity!" cried all the animals. "Why didn't we think of that? Quick! Quick! There's a wind rising now!" And away they rushed, to find hats of their own.

There was a mad scramble

Chapter Four

HATS FOR ALL

You never saw such a cheerful band of animals come trooping down the hill! The most timid of creatures, who would never normally dare to show themselves, went marching into the village. The most nervous of animals, who once upon a time thought that scarecrows were monstrous men, went right into the farmer's field and sat down in front of the scarecrow and waited and watched for the wind to blow.

They did not have to wait long.

A wild west wind whipped over the wheat fields and whirled the hats off a dozen scarecrows. Then, as each hat bowled along the ground, there was a mad scramble to catch it. Everyone wanted a hat to wear to the wedding.

"I'm first!"

"I touched it before you!"

"But I jumped on it!"

"And it's just my size!"

Meanwhile, in the village, the west wind whipped off the hats of a dozen villagers.

"Oh me oh my!" cried Mr Baker the butcher. "There goes my hat!"

"Oh my oh me!" cried Mr Butcher the baker. "There goes mine, too!"

But though they ran fast and looked hard, their hats seemed to have blown clean away. There was not a brim or a crown or a feather or a band to be found.

Out on the road, Mr Driver the driver snatched at his cap, but all he found in his hands was his hair. Mrs Market saw the cap roll into a ditch, but when she searched, she could not find it. And when she got back to her bicycle, her own bonnet was gone. "That must have blown away, too!" she said.

But you know better, don't you?

Whenever the wind blows, it tosses the treetops and it licks up the leaves and it makes waves on the pond and it rattles the doors and windows. It blows the washing off wash-lines – or how else would Sabrina Squirrel have got her wedding dress? And it blows hats off heads – or how else would the animals of Brambledown have found themselves hats that windy afternoon?

Hoppity Hare sat on the top of his hill and watched them with his sharp brown eyes. It was very funny to see such a racing and a chasing, such a snatching and a catching, such a jumping and a thumping. In short, he had never seen such hatting as went on that day in Brambledown.

"Hoppity-woppity! I forgot *me*!" exclaimed the mad March hare, and off he went to find a hat for himself.

Whenever the wind blows

Not easy

It was not easy.

Some of the hats were big, and some of the animals were very small. They had to run very fast to catch up with their hats, and then they had to hold on with teeth and paws and tail.

Some of the hats were not very smart – especially the ones borrowed from scarecrows.

And some of the hats did not fit very well.

"There's nowhere to put my ears," complained Mrs Brown. "Should I leave them on the outside or fold them away inside?"

"My hat's rather *small*," said Harry the Horse.

"And my hat's rather *big*," said Fergus Field-Mouse as he climbed inside it and walked about. "And it's very dark inside here."

"... dark inside here"

"No matter! No matter!" said Hoppity Hare. "Hoppity-wop-pity! What do you want for free? If your hat is too small it will stretch. And if it's too big, it will shrink in the rain. And Mrs Brown, you can wear one ear inside the hat one ear outside. That's very fashionable for weddings!"

"Where am I?" asked Fergus, his squeak muffled inside the hat.

"Half way between this morning and tonight," Hoppity Hare told him, unhelpfully.

"I remember! I'm on my way to the Squirrels' wedding . . . But that's not until tomorrow."

So Fergus Field-Mouse curled up inside his new hat and went to sleep. It was really very comfortable, and he was well out of the draughts. He would be quite rested by the morning.

"It will shrink"

Just then, Henry Hedgehog came by, wearing his new hat.

"Hi Henry!" called the other animals. "Look at us! Look at us!"

But Henry was feeling much too grand to look at other people, and he swaggered on by, his pink nose pointing so high in the air that he could not see his friends or their strange collection of hats. If he had he would have been most amused.

"Hoity-toity! Who's a haughty hedgehog in a high hat?" called out Maurice Mole in his most teasing voice.

But all Henry said in reply was, "Herrumph!"

(To tell the truth, he did look a lot smarter than the others, because he had not come by his hat on a windy day.)

The scarecrows said nothing

But then *everybody* pushed their pink noses in the air and walked home in their hats. They stumbled over stones, they fell over fir-cones, they tripped over tree roots. But they felt just as grand as grand can be.

Of course, Mr Butcher and Mr Baker and Mr Driver and Mrs Market all had to go home without their hats.

The farmers out driving their tractors through the fields saw each tousled scarecrow and thought, "Bother! The wind has blown off his hat. I must find him another one!"

But what the scarecrows thought about it, I don't know, because they said nothing at all. They just stood there, with their big coats flapping, and their heads bare.

The leaves of the trees trembled with excitement. The moon refused to set when morning came. The sun came up especially early. Because everybody in Brambledown wanted to be there at the wedding of Sam and Sabrina Squirrel.

Everybody dressed for the occasion

Chapter Five

THE WEDDING

Next day all the guests assembled for the big event. Everyone who lived in woods or orchard or field or pond set off from their homes for the wedding.

The spot was a sunny, grassy slope near the pond in Brambledown Wood. That is where The Wedding Tree stands – a cherry all covered in white and pink blossom that looked just like confetti.

All the guests came early, because nobody wanted to be at the back and miss seeing the bride and groom. Some brought presents and some brought flowers and some brought food for the party afterwards. And everybody came dressed for the occasion, in their best spring coats and, of course, their strange collection of new-found hats.

Fergus fell in

Fergus Field-Mouse was rather wet. Walking along inside his big hat, not able to see where he was going, he had fallen into a puddle.

Barney Brown (who is always leaping and bounding and bouncing and jumping) had leaped one bounce too many and jumped his head right through his hat, so he was wearing it round his neck.

High in the trees, the birds sang a song to welcome the bride and groom and in came Sam and Sabrina. They were so shy and happy, they did not even notice how odd their guests looked. The Magpie, in his black feathers and white collar, spoke a few solemn words, and then declared that the two were married – and everybody cheered.

Paw-in-paw, the happy pair walked down the grassy slope and the photographer set up his camera.

That was when the trouble began.

Henry Hedgehog, feeling so grand in his high hat, decided that he ought to be in the front of the picture.

"Hoi! Henry! You're not the most important guest!" cried Barney Brown.

"Herrumph!" said Henry, and he went and stood right between the bride and groom, throwing petals in the air.

"Well!" said Maurice Mole.

"Well!" said Mrs Brown.

"We-gg-le! We-gg-le!" said Oggie the Frog.

"Hoppity-woppity!" said the Hare. And then everybody tried to be in the front for the wedding photographs.

There was such a commotion that poor Sam and Sabrina couldn't be seen at all.

Barney gave Henry a push. But that can be a very painful thing to do – to push a hedgehog! His paw full of prickles, he bounced about and tripped over Maurice Mole who was creeping slyly to the front on all-fours.

Bounder Brown the rabbit popped up in front of the camera and grinned into the lens. Henry the Horse pulled Bounder's hat down over his grin.

"Hey! What happened? It's all gone dark!" cried Bounder, and wandered away with outstretched paws.

Fergus Field-Mouse, roaming about inside his hat squeaked, "What's going on? I can't see!" and got under everyone's feet and tripped them up.

Clean through his hat

Hoppity Hare pranced about like a boxer, paws up: "Hoppity-woppity! Hoppity-woppity!" Then he bounced clean out through the top of his hat.

"Please! Quiet! Calm down everybody! Please!" whistled Mr Magpie. But no-one could hear him stamping his tiny foot.

In the end, the photographer was tumbled into the pond.

There were hats jumped on,
there were hats thumped on.
There were hats coshed
and there were hats squashed.
There were hats swopped
and there were hats whopped.

In the end, Mr Wise-Owl was sent for to restore peace and order.

When the animals picked themselves up and dusted themselves down, they discovered that the bride and groom had crept quietly away to the top of the tallest tree. The wedding was all over. The food was spilled, the flowers were spoiled, the presents were squirrelled away.

The creatures gathered up their different, dusty hats and crammed them on their different, dusty heads. There was nothing to do but to go home, and they set off in a dozen different directions from The Wedding Tree for their burrows, lairs, nests and dens in and around Brambledown.

The choir of birds looked down from their branches and laughed. There was plenty to laugh at: hares and horses in hats, chickens and cats in caps, bunnies in bonnets, moles all muffled up and badgers blinkered, because they had all wanted to wear high hats and look grand.

Plenty to laugh at

The animals of Brambledown bumbled home, balancing their bent hats on their aching heads. They did not look or feel very grand now. They felt battered and bruised and sulky and silly.

They said, "It's Henry Hedgehog's fault!"

"Henry started it!"

"Henry is to blame, and Henry's hat."

". . . by the way, where *is* Henry?"

Nobody knew.

Nobody saw him go.

They were all so busy quarrelling and pushing and squabbling and falling over. They did not see Henry stride grandly away, as soon as the trouble began. He pointed his pink nose in the air, as haughty as ever, and still wearing his handsome high hat on the back of his head, he swaggered out of sight.

(Of course Bounder Brown saw less than anybody, because his hat was still pulled over his eyes.)

Next day, Henry Hedgehog was still strutting about the woods and orchards and fields as proud as ever. Whenever anyone spoke to him, you know the answer they got.

"Herrumph!"

They threw away their own hats and they decided Henry's hat must go, too. No doubt about it. Henry's hat had to go. They had all had enough.

...pulled over his eyes

"Remember how we got our hats?"

Chapter Six

HATS OFF!

"But how are we to get Henry's hat away from him?" said Maurice Mole. "He wears it all day and hides it at night."

They asked Mr Wise-Owl, but he only said, "Who knows? Who knows?"

"That's what *we* asked *you*." At last they climbed High Hill to talk to Hoppity Hare. "How can we stop Henry being so haughty and saying 'Herrumph'? We liked him the way he was *before* the hat."

Hoppity sat so still for so long that everybody thought he had gone to sleep. But just as they began to creep away he opened his eyes and leaped up: "I've thought about it and I think I have the answer."

"And?"

"Do you remember how we got our hats?"

"Of course. Of course," said Barney Brown impatiently. "We waited for a windy day and then we . . . ah! I see what you mean!"

Now Barney Brown the rabbit has a very large family. He gathered round him all his children and grandchildren and he told them just what they had to do.

That day and every day after that, the little Brown rabbits followed Henry Hedgehog about.

"What a fine hat, Henry!"

"How grand you look in it!"

"Where did you get it, Henry?"

"If we are good, can we have hats like it when we grow up?"

Of course they got only one answer from Henry:

"Herrumph!"

He felt far too grand, in his high hat, to speak to small rabbits. But the little Brown rabbits kept on following Henry about and saying nice things about his hat.

Then along came a windy day.

Henry went out as usual to walk about wearing his hat. The little Brown rabbits went out, too, to follow him and admire his hat. Of course, Henry had *not* listened to the advice of Fenella and Fergus Field-Mouse. He had *not* attached strings or ribbons to his hat to tie under his chin.

So when a gust of wind snatched it off his head he tried to catch hold, he tried to catch it!

A gust of wind

But the hat bowled and rolled away from him.

"It's all right! Never fear! We'll get it back for you, Uncle Henry" shrieked the little Brown rabbits.

Away they bounded, as fast and helpful as can be, to chase the windy hat along the blowy path and over the breezy field.

"I've got it!" shouted one. "Oops! I dropped it."

"I've caught it!" cried another. "No, there it goes again."

"Don't let it get away!" wailed a third, and flung himself on it, squashing it flat.

"Hold it tight!" shouted one, taking a grip of the crown.

"I've got it safe now!" cried another and closed his teeth on the brim.

"We've stopped your hat blowing away, Uncle Henry!" squealed the little Brown rabbits, all sitting on the hat.

When they gave it back to Henry, he stared at it in horror. "Look what you've done to my hat! You've squashed it and crushed it and crumpled it and rumpled it and sat on it and flattened it!"

"But we did stop it blowing away, didn't we, Uncle Henry? . . . And how nice it is to hear you say something different from 'Herrumph!'"

Henry could not wear his hat after that. So he did not have any reason to walk about with his nose in the air, feeling grand. In fact he felt no different from the other animals, so he stopped saying, "Herrumph" to them and started to say "Good morning" again. His friends were so happy that they never tried to tell him how horrid he had been in his high hat. Instead they made sure he knew how much they liked him without it. And summer was coming, so who needed a hat?

Flattened

The Bramb